Be An Author

-

What Would It Be Like If...
You Write Your Book?

Anne Orchard

British Library Cataloguing in Publication Data: A Catalogue record for this book is available from The British Library.

ISBN Number: 978-0-9556906-5-5

First edition published by:

Crystal Clear Books,
West View,
West Street,
Broadwindsor,
Beaminster,
Dorset,
DT8 3QQ,
United Kingdom

Note/Disclaimer: The material contained in this book is set out in good faith for general guidance and no liability can be accepted for loss or expense incurred in relying on the information given.

Cover Image: Colorful Books © Jarihin | Dreamstime.com

For my husband Pete,
who has been behind everything I have done

Contents

1

Before We Begin

... in which we meet our contributing authors
and make sure you are ready to get started.

This is not a 'how to' book. You won't find details of writing or publishing techniques. What you will find is the answers to questions you might have and resources to help you move forward. I don't know where you are in your writing project, but the chances are that you have hit some kind of a stumbling block. You aren't the first person to do so, and you won't be the last. In this book I share insights and advice from other authors who have gone before (and some of what I have learned along the way as well). Before we begin, I want to introduce you to our contributors, so that you know whose voices you will be hearing.

Sallyann Sheridan

Sallyann's background is as a copywriter. She has written advertising copy for national companies, book cover text for publishing houses, and then moved on to writing for herself. She has written a number of non-fiction books including *The Magic of Writing Things Down*, numerous stories and feature articles for magazines and in 2009 her first novel, *If Wishes Were Horses*, was published. Her lastest book *Relax* is available as a download from her website with its companion relaxation audio *Let Go*. You can find out more about Sallyann at **www.sallyannsheridan.com**.

Simon Hall

Simon Hall is a crime reporter for BBC TV in the South West. Intrigued by the similar skills required in journalism and police work, Simon created the 'TV Detective', and has written a series of mysteries involving this character.

Simon self-published his first book, before securing a publisher for the subsequent books. Simon still works full time and regards writing and promoting his books (one of which has now been adapted into a stage play) as one of life's great pleasures. Simon can be found online at **www.thetvdetective.com**.

Wendy Knee

Wendy is a life coach, adventurer and inspiration to all who know her. Having lived a full life with many ups and downs, Wendy came to writing in her sixties with a little book called *Never Die Wondering*. This book continues to enjoy success – and to change people's lives – and has since been joined by a companion, *Get Cracking*.

Wendy is now working on *Travels with Granny* – the story of both her own travels and how she is sharing that love of adventure with her grandchildren. See more **at www.wendyknee.com**.

What you read will act as a catalyst to propel your project forwards.

Linda Parkinson-Hardman

Linda's writing came out of her social enterprise The Hysterectomy Association. Having done research which showed that women given information do better after hysterectomy and that this information was not widely available, Linda plugged the gap with her online support. This was followed by several books on the subject including *101 Handy Hints for a Happy Hysterectomy*.

Harnessing the Internet in its early days, Linda also knows more than most about all things web related. She now teaches and consults on web-based business. Her latest non-fiction book *LinkedIn Made Easy* helps you get the most out of the most prominent business social network. Linda has now branched into fiction with her first novel, *Woman on the Edge of Reality*. Linda can be found online in several places including **www.womanontheedgeofreality.com**.

Using this book

Now you know who your guides will be, it is time to get started. But first I want you to pick up a pen, pencil or whatever technology you use instead. This is meant to be a working book. Although it won't tell you exactly what to do, there is plenty of wisdom contained here. While you are reading, you will be making connections with your own situation. Ideas will come to you and I want you to capture them straight away before they flit off, crowded out by the busy-ness of life. Make lots of notes, whether they are on paper or digital, and what you read will act as a catalyst to propel your project forwards.

2

Introduction

… in which we think about writers
who have gone before, and how
reading this book can help you.

"Times are bad. Children no longer obey their parents, and everyone is writing a book."

- Marcus Tullius Cicero

If you've picked up this book, the chances are you are one of the many who want to write, but feel frustrated at not having achieved that goal. You may feel quite isolated, fed up with yourself and your inablity to get your book out. Or perhaps you are tempted to give up on your dream, thinking "It's not for the likes of me to achieve fame and fortune."

You hear interviews with celebrity authors about how they got their break, and you think that the same could never happen for you. After all, many of them started writing years ago, before the publishing industry underwent a seismic shift with the rise of print-on-demand and the ease of self-publishing. Many of them were famous before they wrote their books - and generated sales on the back of that celebrity. So where does that leave you if you are not already famous? Is it too late to become the next big thing? Is it easier to give up?

It would be easier. Oh yes, then you could spend long evenings comforting yourself that it was all just too difficult. But what if the truth is that it *can* be done. That people just like you are getting their books into print - even finding major publishers?

As part of the research for this book, I asked people to complete the sentence 'I think I would like to write a book but...' and the answers were quite fascinating. They weren't along the lines of 'but...I don't have a degree' or '...I haven't studied creative writing' or even '...it's all too hard'.

No, what is holding people back is fear. Fear that what they have to say would not be good enough, or somehow worthy of publication. Even those who say 'but...I just can't find the time' don't really mean it. They mean '...I haven't given it a high enough priority...yet'.

I'm going to let you into a secret. All those other people who have published or self-published their books didn't have the time either. They also had fears, and yet something inspired them to carry on and overcome the obstacles. And so that you can't use the excuse that these are somehow exalted beings living in a different stratosphere to you, I've deliberately not talked to mega-celebrity authors. These are people just like you and me. They did what it takes to get *their* book out. And then the next one. And the one after that. They did what they had to do to get their books noticed and guess what? It took them time and effort. But now they are where you could be in a few years time, or less.

In these pages you will find the real story of what it's like in today's world, to write, print and promote a book. You will see that it is possible - that you can do it too. You will even find realism about what you will have to do, and how you will grow in the process. Perhaps you will decide it's all too much for you, that your passions lie elsewhere, and that voice which tells you to write will be stilled. If so, that is not a problem, just an opportunity to turn to other interests.

On the other hand, if that voice is still there at the end perhaps it will have become louder and more insistent. Perhaps you will take the first step and then the next towards realising your dream. I hope so! Someone out there needs to hear what you have to say. They can only appreciate the message (or enjoy the entertainment) in the way you can express it.

Will your book be a success? Who knows? I certainly don't; I don't even know how you define what success might be to you. It may be that the market will have to decide. But you will have the satisfaction of putting your creativity to work in the service of others. What better life could there be?

> In these pages you will find the real story of what it's like in today's world to write, print and promote a book.

"When once the itch of literature comes over a man, nothing can cure it but the scratching of a pen."

- Samuel Lover

3

Getting Started

... in which we find out how our
authors got their first ideas, and
what motivated them to take action.

> "What is not started today is never finished tomorrow"
>
> - Johann Wolfgang Goethe

"The idea is everything."

- Simon

For many people the idea of writing a book is just that – an idea. You feel you have something to say, and maybe you've enjoyed writing some pieces before. But the big one is proving elusive. Maybe you know you want to write a novel, but what genre? Perhaps you are keen on self-help books but worried that everything you know has been said before. So how do you get off the starting block? Let's turn to our contributing authors to find out how it was for them.

"Where did you first get the idea to write a book?"

Simon : The idea is everything. Mine came when I was talking to a detective about the similarities between the role of journalist and cop - in essence, ask the right questions, read the reactions, get to the hidden truth. From that, came the idea of a TV reporter who covers crimes, and gets so involved in the cases, he ends up helping to solve them.

Wendy : Through working as a life coach and wanting to have a product for clients to take home.

Linda : I'd been thinking about a book to complement the Hysterectomy Association website for some time and it was really the title that came first, *101 Handy Hints for a Happy Hysterectomy* – after I got that it took me another two years to actually write it.

Sallyann : I was asked to write booklets as a copywriter, and I was commissioned to write my first book *Using Relaxation for Health and Success* because it was my area of experience. The publisher only published books from people who were writers and also experienced in their field.

I have written short fiction for years for magazines and in 1995 I wrote my first full-length book. I didn't continue with it at that time because the idea of being a novelist felt like an indulgence rather than a way of earning a living.

For some the idea comes fully formed, for others it seems to be a progression out of work they are doing already. In my case, I had wanted to write a book for years as a way of generating long-term income while I slept! That idea on its own, though, was never quite enough to get me started.

I was always clear to me that I would write non-fiction, but it took time to settle on the subject. Others know their subject right from having the first idea.

One of the most basic divisions between books is whether they are fiction or non-fiction. Our authors had a varied approach to finding out which they wanted to write, and what their subject would be.

"How did you know what to write about and whether to write fiction or non-fiction?"

Linda : I had recently started The Hysterectomy Association and was already writing about hysterectomy, so a non-fiction book was almost guaranteed. It was based on the numbers of questions I kept getting by email from women who were using the website.

Simon : I think it all comes from that central, first idea. It guides you - and it should be your passion, something you can truly believe in. Otherwise, you'll never make a book convincing, be it fiction or non, and it's highly unlikely you'll even finish writing it.

I agree with Simon that your book subject should be something you feel passionate about. Only then will people want to hear you talk about it (which you are going to have to do). And only then will you be prepared to live with your creation in the years to come. It's going to be like a child to you, so you must want to nurture it into the future.

"I felt I
had to
make a big
leap."

- Wendy

My approach to settling on the idea was to play with it. My book was only one of a number of ideas for that potential long-term income which popped into my head. What I did was to buy a 'Dream Book' – a beautiful journal with plain paper pages. Then I created a page in the book for each of those ideas and noted down anything that occurred to me. I sat in the garden or my conservatory – anywhere that induced creativity rather than restriction. For the book project, my first idea was to write about the creation of my local hospice – Blythe House Hospice in the High Peak – as I thought it was a fascinating story. I loved the place and the ethos of how it was run.

That was my start – not really writing, but writing down ideas and inspiration as they came.

Ideas are one thing; completion of a project is quite another. Even getting started can be a major challenge. So what affects the transition from inspiration to action? What made our authors take that brave first step?

What do you think made the difference between it being an idea and actually doing it?

Wendy: I felt I had to make a big leap – do something in order to forward my work. It put me on a new level to promote myself.

Sallyann: In relation to writing my novel - I was going through a rough patch, and realised that fiction had given me as much help as non-fiction in getting through that. That made me feel that fiction was just as valid as writing self-help books and that seemed to open the floodgates to writing my first published novel.

Linda: Leaving my job and deciding that I was going to work full time on The Hysterectomy Association – one of those 'now or never' moments and the thought that I might regret it if I didn't do it.

Simon : It's all down to belief. You've got to have an idea that enthuses you; that you can make live. One that you carry around with you, that's never far from your thoughts and that you can't wait to set down on paper. It may sound odd, but it's like a relationship. You have to have love for your subject to make it work. And if you do, it'll love you back.

I took the step from the idea to 'doing it' because I had an outside influence – my own life coach. She knew about my dream book and the idea of writing a book – even that it had some relationship to cancer because that was what my mother had died from. So she challenged me to start researching books on cancer – to see what was out there. I well remember the conversation that flipped the switch for me. I said to her "The trouble is that books about cancer are written by people who have survived cancer themselves, or people who work with cancer patients. I don't have that kind of authority, but I will tell you what I do know. I know what it is like to be a family member – to sit on the sidelines not knowing how to help or who is going to help me!" That was it. As soon as I knew who the book was for, I knew I absolutely had to write it – the passion had arrived.

There is definitely something magical about getting started. Once your project is real – even if you have only bought a journal like I did – your subconscious mind will go to work on it. I find this if I have to give a speech, or I start on a new project like this book. Once I've actually got going, it begins to write itself in my head – whether I like it or not!

"Twenty years from now you will be more disappointed with the things that you didn't do than by the ones you did do. So throw off the bowline. Sail away from the safe harbour. Catch the trade winds in your sails. Explore, Dream. Discover."

- Mark Twain

4

Goals

… in which we consider the goals our
authors set for their writing, and
whether they changed over time.

"If you want to be happy, set a goal that commands your thoughts, liberates your energy and inspires your hopes."

- Andrew Carnegie

Goals are a thorny subject. Some people have many goals, ambitions they want to achieve in their lifetime. Maybe writing a book is one of yours – but why? What do you want to achieve with your book, and what do you want your book to achieve for you?

Other people have the feeling that setting goals creates too much pressure. Maybe you are setting yourself up for failure and the challenges that can bring. But those with the opposite approach might say that by *not* setting goals you are guaranteeing failure because you will have no incentive to put in the time needed to accomplish anything.

What approach did our authors use – did they set themselves goals when they first set out to write?

What goal did you originally have for your books and / or writing?

Simon : A very modest one - to see if I could do it. It was a personal challenge. When I wrote the first book, only then did I approach an agent. I was amazed when he took it on, stunned when people began to read the books, and utterly poleaxed that they wanted more.

Wendy : My goals were to reach a wider audience, and have something for people to take home after a seminar or talk as a guide and prompt.

Linda : I have different goals. One is to make enough money to support the Hysterectomy Association. Another is to increase my level of exposure in the business world. But they are all driven by a need to communicate information to people to help them make the most of their health and happiness.

Sallyann : As a copywriter, my goal was to make a living by doing something that I was good at and that would make a difference. The goal for my novel was to write something worthy of publication – beyond that it was for at least one person to take away a message from the book that improved their life (even if that was just taking them out of their life for a time).

These may not be the lofty ideals you might have imagined! For myself I did set a goal – and a big one. I wanted to sell a million copies of my book *Their Cancer – Your Journey*, and I still do. But I know that I underestimated what would be involved in that, and the effort it would take. It also led me to invest perhaps too much money in the early stages – but more of that later (See **Traditional Publishing vs Self-Publishing**).

What goal might you set for your book? Make notes of any ideas you have now. You can continue to work on them later.

My goal to sell a million copies of my book is still there, though I acknowledge that I have no idea what timescale that might happen over. Writing this book, however, I found that my goals were very different because of my earlier experiences. So what has been the case with our authors? Have their goals stayed as they were, or changed as time has gone by?

Has that goal changed over time?

Simon : Yes. I can now look - albeit a long way ahead - to making significant sums of money and perhaps even becoming a full time writer. But I don't think you should do that from the start, it makes for too much pressure, which is unhealthy and unnecessary. Begin by doing it for yourself and see where it takes you. Consider anything else a bonus.

Sallyann : As I continue with my next novel, I would still like to think it would be well-written. I also love

> "Begin by doing it for yourself and see where it takes you."
>
> - Simon

getting feedback from people saying that reading my book had given them pleasure, so I would like to get more of that.

Don't get me wrong, financial reward would be great, but that was never my reason for turning to fiction writing.

Linda : As I have written more, I have developed as an author. As I've developed I have been exposed to other opportunities. So yes, my goals are changing all the time.

Wendy : The goal is also to have follow-on books.

So Simon is now thinking in terms of making a living as an author. Wendy now knows she enjoys the process of creating a book, and that she has developed skills to sell them. So she now has a goal to continue creating books. My goals for this book were to write something completely different so that I do not always have to write about illness; to try out a way of writing which involves contribution from others; and to support my work with the Charmouth Literary Festival. Nothing about numbers sold, and no large investment. I am now much more like Simon was originally – let's just see what I can do with it.

Your goals may also change as time goes by, but that doesn't mean there is no point in setting any at all. I am reminded of the quote from Dwight D. Eisenhower that 'plans are nothing, planning is everything'. Perhaps it is necessary to set some goals just so you can alter them as you get feedback from the world about your writing. At least it gives you something to aim for.

"Far away there in the sunshine are my highest aspirations. I may not reach them, but I can look up and see their beauty, believe in them, and try to follow where they lead."

- Louisa May Alcott

5

Traditional Publishing
vs
Self-Publishing

... in which we look at the pros and cons
of each approach and why our authors
took the route they did

> "Most writers have totally unrealistic concepts of how publishing works."
>
> - Jim Harrison

One of the big fear factors in writing a book is what happens next?

One of the big fear factors involved in writing a book is what happens next? You have probably heard that it is very hard to get published; that the Harry Potter books had been rejected many times before a publisher was prepared to take a risk on them. You may realise that the publishing world has changed dramatically with the rise of ePublishing. You may know that it is possible to self-publish your book, but wonder if this is really such a good idea. How would you know how to go about it, or what is involved?

It might help to start by thinking about the business of publishing – and it is a business. For mainstream publishers, the reality is that only a few of the books they print will make them money. Unfortunately for them it is very difficult to predict which ones those will be, so their risk on any one book is quite high. They can reduce this risk by taking books from authors with a proven sales record, or those who already have a degree of celebrity. Books from new authors represent the highest risk to a publisher.

In self-publishing all the risk to you falls onto that one first book, although if you find a way to keep going and produce several books you can spread that risk yourself. Many of the most successful self-publishers have a background in marketing, so if you do not have those skills already gaining them may be a priority. Another way to reduce the risk in self-publishing is to keep costs low – then fewer sales will be required to cover those costs and get your book into profit.

This is where my cautionary tale fits of over-spending on my book. Because of my lofty ambitions for *Their Cancer – Your Journey* I spent money on getting help with the skills I did not have in order to have a professional product to self-publish. This was not too much of a problem. What did turn out to be a problem was having too many copies printed because I believed I would be able to sell them in quantity through the many existing cancer charities and support groups. I just did not understand how these organisations worked, and that marketing route never took off. This left me with a large print run that I am still in the process of shifting, at a loss to me.

This is a risk you don't have to take with the benefit of my hindsight! You can take the approach I would now use in the same position, using a print-on-demand company to print a few books at a time and testing every marketing route to see which ones work.

Read on to learn more about the pros and cons of these two contrasting ways of getting your book to its readers. Our authors have taken a variety of routes to get their books to the public, as you will see:

How did you decide whether to self-publish or find a mainstream publisher?

Simon : If possible, always go with a mainstream publisher. They've got the support, expertise and marketing to help you. Plus there's more money in it. But don't be afraid of self-publishing - it can give you a product to show around, to talk about, and a foundation from which to find a mainstream publisher.

Sallyann : I have had experience of both – and good experiences on both side. There are pros and cons with either and the best approach depends on the individual book.

Linda : That was easy because you would never find a book on Hysterectomy in a bookshop, which meant that the market would be limited and therefore unlikely that a publisher would be interested. By self-publishing it meant that almost all the RRP goes to the Association rather than the various third parties involved. I set The Hysterectomy Association up as a publisher itself instead.

So there are many factors involved, and it may well be that you end up doing both. Certainly for many, self-publishing is a step on the way to mainstream publishing.

"There are pros and cons with either [traditional or self-publishing] and the best approach depends on the individual book."

- Sallyann

In my case, I was originally determined to find a mainstream publisher. This was partly a result of the enormous goal I told you about in the last chapter. I felt that a traditional publisher had the best chance of helping me to achieve this, naively believing that if a publisher believed in my book that they would put considerable marketing muscle behind it. Hmm.

For those who feel that mainstream publishing is the way for you, let's check in with our authors about what that meant for them.

What are the positives and pitfalls of working with a mainstream publisher?

Sallyann : Positives are that they take a lot of the strain of the marketing and PR – though of course you can't rely on them completely and still have to do lots yourself. The downside is the time it takes to appear on the shelves.

Simon : The positives are the expertise, support and marketing they provide, plus the ability to get your book in the shops and online. The downside is that it's a ruthless business. As a newcomer, you're likely to be bottom of their list of priorities, and if you don't sell decent amounts of books quickly, you can get dumped again very fast. It's hard to recover from that.

There's an interesting word that Simon uses in his response there. He said if *you* don't sell decent amounts of books. Well, it may just be a figure of speech, but my understanding was that the publisher was going to sell (i.e. promote) the books. Perhaps it is not as simple as all that, though. Perhaps your efforts will be what determine whether your book will sink or swim.

Bearing in mind the advantages, then, how much of your life do you need to set aside if a mainstream publisher is your aim? Simon shares how long the process took for him.

How long did it take you to find a publisher?

Simon: About three years. Never believe these "overnight success" stories you see in the press - I know, I'm a hack! It's always much more complex than that. Writing is a trade, like any other. You have to serve an apprenticeship, practice and build up your talents before you get good enough to be paid for it.

From my experience this is fairly typical. Many authors I have met spent several years (*after* writing their book, mind you) sending the manuscript round to agents or publishers. This includes Brandon Mull, the author of the popular children's Fablehaven series.

This time element is the reason why I ended up self-publishing. I had found an agent who wanted to represent my book, and he was taking it out to publishers. Expecting some to say "no", the rejections did not bother me too much. What did, though, was the time that my book was sitting partly written. My agent had advised me that for a non-fiction book you should not write the whole manuscript until you had a publisher, as they might want to direct the content of the book. So with a partial manuscript and nothing much happening, I was challenged by a friend to begin writing again - which led me onto a different path.

So if you set aside the time and are persistent, you may find a publisher for your book. But you may have to cope with setbacks along the way.

Did you experience any rejection and if so how did you handle that?

Simon : Yep, and you should expect it and not let it get to you. JK Rowling got loads of rejections, as did The Beatles. I don't know any author who hasn't. Remember this - it's by far easier, and actually, a reflex action, for a publisher to say no. It means no work and no effort for them. Just take it with a smile and don't be deterred - keep trying.

You can indeed keep trying and some will be happy to do this, continuing to send their book out time and time again as they do the rounds of publishers and/or agents. Or you can decide that you believe in your book enough to publish it yourself. Several of our authors did this - some for all their books so far, some as an initial step and a springboard which has led them into the mainstream publishing world.

If you are self-publishing, you may already have all the skills you need, or you may need to develop some along the way. How was this for our contributors?

What skills do you think you had (or developed) that made you successful in self-publishing your books?

Wendy: I was determined about the layout of the book, developed a lot of courage in talking to bookshops. I overcame financial restraints and there was the skill of remaining positive throughout.

Simon: You need energy, commitment and determination - because no one will do it for you. You've got to go out to the media and libraries and sell yourself. Build up an interest in your work so you can demonstrate that to a mainstream publisher. Save articles, posters about your talks, anything that might impress, and send them in any future applications to other publishers. Take any edge you can get.

Linda: Editing definitely, and I already had reasonably good levels of skills when it came to putting the various files together to make the finished book. I also had a ready-made marketplace to act as a springboard.

Sallyann: My background in marketing and copywriting was really useful. I am happy to talk to people and phone bookshops, newspapers etc. It was harder, though, to promote my own book rather than a product I had been hired to market – that thin line you have to tread of belief in your book as opposed to arrogance.

There are many skills needed for self-publishing, but you don't necessarily have to have them all yourself! I paid for some professional tasks such as a book cover design, professional editing - and had the benefit of a techno-savvy husband who learned about book formatting and laid out the inside of the book for me. Far and away the hardest skills for me to gain have been those regarding promotion of my book, which we will cover in greater depth in a later chapter (**Getting The Word Out**).

How did you develop the skills you needed?

> **Sallyann:** I had to toughen myself up through practice, as some bookshops could be anti self-publishing in the past – though I think this is changing.
>
> **Linda:** Years of experience writing and editing for different types of reader and audience. So I guess just doing it rather than any formal training.
>
> **Wendy:** Talking to others who had done digital printing, and printing companies, and those who had self-published before.

The skills I did acquire were learned from others who had already self-published. There were also plenty of books that came in handy, which you will find in our resources section at the end of the book.

You may be thinking that this all seems like a huge amount of work. How did our authors cope with the demands of self-publishing?

Weren't you put off by the energy needed in order to self-publish?

> **Simon:** Yes, it is daunting. But if you believe, and there's no other way, then do it. The belief will carry you through.

> **Linda:** To me, it seemed a lot less energy than the amount I'd need to put in to getting it in front of potential agents and publishers. I'm more of a 'can do' person than a 'sit back and wait for someone to reject me' person.

> **Sallyann:** I used an approach for one of my books called partnership publishing, which meant that the publisher would help with some of the marketing, the book design and knowing what was involved. This approach worked well for me. As the book continued to sell, the arrangement with the publisher means that they continue to print the book and I get a much higher royalty than with traditional publishing.

It was Linda who inspired me to believe it was possible, and I felt my book was important enough to give it a go myself. Given the time it can take to get a book known (I have read that it takes 3-5 years for a book to reach its true potential through word of mouth) I think the sooner it is in print, the better!

Then once your book is in print, you need to make sure that people are able to buy it.

Did you find it easy to get your self-published book distributed?

> **Simon:** No, but you have to keep pushing and keep trying. If you do, eventually you'll make progress.

> **Wendy:** No, it wasn't easy. Most bookshops want to go through a recognised distributor, so from that point of view selling the book yourself is hard work. Getting on Amazon Advantage program has helped.

Sallyann: The partnership publishing approach made this much easier as they set up all the distribution channels.

Linda: As I already had a well used website this wasn't as much of a struggle as it might have been. It is distributed by the online bookshops. To get it into the US was harder and for that I used an online print-on-demand company. The only problem is that in the UK the book appears twice in the Amazon listings at two different prices....! I also receive orders from independent bookstores, either directly or most usually through Gardners. The libraries stock through Bertrams. Having an account with Nielsens has helped enormously for this. (Note: there are explanations of the terms Linda uses here and more information about how books are distributed in the **Resources** section)

Distribution is a big factor - perhaps especially for fiction. Few bookshops will take a book directly from a self-published author - it just isn't cost-effective for them in terms of time. However it is easy these days to get on the lists for bookshops to order your book - but you have to drive the people into the bookstore to ask for it through your own efforts.

It may also be worth looking at how people who like to read books in your genre tend to buy their books. In my case, because my book related to cancer, I found that bookshops just don't carry that kind of book anyway (I was told that the subject is too depressing). So distribution to bookshops was not a major factor in my case. The online distribution was all handled by Lulu, the print-on-demand company I used, so my book is available in all online bookstores. I just had to get the book known.

For those of you who are not prepared to play the waiting game, let's just check how to get your book out quickly.

"Publishing is a mysterious business. It is hard to predict what kind of sale or reception a book will have, and advertising seems to do very little good."

- Thomas Wolfe

What is the fastest way to get your book published and available?

> **Wendy:** Use a recommended local printer, or add it to Lulu or Lightning Source. The very fastest way is to make it available as an eBook.

> **Linda:** Definitely online print-on-demand with a distribution account.

As I said before, speed does make a difference. There are also lots of precedents for self-published books or eBooks making their way into major publishers' lists. The reason for this is that the publishers only have to consider books that are already selling well. This may seem a strange idea - surely then the publisher would have missed out on sales made already. But we've already had a look at the way mainstream publishing works. Most of the books produced by a publishing house will not sell well - they will in fact make a loss for the publisher.

However the few books that do really well make up the profit. Taking a tried and tested book - one that has shown good and increasing sales and has not yet reached its full potential - can reduce the risk for a publisher considerably. An example of this is *The Christmas Box* - the first book by Richard Paul Evans. He self-published the book and sold several hundred thousand copies of his own edition before it was republished by Simon and Schuster. The book then went on to sell several million copies, as have Richard's further books.

The decision is down to you. If you are really not prepared to go it alone (and it can be a lonely business), then the traditional publishing route still works. Do consider self-publishing though. It can be a school of hard knocks, but you will learn some astonishing skills. The most unexpected people may champion your book, and you are quite likely to grow in many ways. Not everyone goes on to be a New York Times bestseller like Richard Paul Evans, but maybe you will.

"Publishing is a business. Writing may be art, but publishing, when all is said and done, comes down to dollars."

- Nicholas Sparks

6

ePublishing

... in which we consider how electronic publishing has changed in recent years and see how our authors feel about the effects on them.

"Technology has changed the way book publishing works, as it has changed everything else in the world of media."

- Bruce Jackson

Since the advent of eReaders, and with the ever present online experience, especially for the younger audience, electronic publishing has begun to take off. There are lots of resources to tell you how to publish electronically, but I wanted to know how our authors really felt about the rise of ePublishing.

First let's find out what ePublishing they have done for their works so far:

What electronic publishing have you (or your publisher) done for your books to date?

Simon: My publisher puts all my books out in e format.

Wendy: I have produced Kindle eBook versions of my first two books.

Sallyann: I have ePublished *Relax*, a self-help book on recognising and dealing effectively with excessive pressure - be it physical or psychological. I also ePublished *Let Go* a daily 20 min deep relaxation session download preceded by 16 suggestions of things to let go of to aid relaxation and contentment.

Linda: I started in the late 1990s with a pdf download of a free booklet. In 2010 all my books were converted by Lulu into formats for ePlatforms. In late 2010 I published my first Kindle books.

So all our authors have at the very least dipped their toe in the ePublishing waters. And so have I. I tried publishing *Their Cancer – Your Journey* as an eBook when it first came out, with very little success. Then it was converted to some of the digital formats by Lulu and I now have some digital sales. I have yet to successfully create a Kindle version though due to issues with the formatting. I am determined to get to the bottom of this, though.

The next question I had was whether our authors' forays into ePublishing were out of choice:

Was your ePublishing a result of your own desire or of feeling obliged in some way?

Linda: I was always aware that I wanted to make my writing as accessible as possible to the widest audience. The original pdfs were created so that women in the US could easily get them without having to pay for international postage and wait for post to arrive.

Sallyann: The two products (*Relax* eBook and *Let Go* relaxation download) are updated versions of my previous books and CDs. They sold well and proved of real benefit so I wanted to update and re-release them. It seemed a logical conclusion where the CD was concerned to re-release as a download. I thought I would try the book as an eBook to aid speed of release and (since I received the rights back from the UK publisher) it was also a more cost effective option for me.

Wendy: I felt obliged to follow the trend.

Simon: It's now become standard – but if it wasn't, I would feel obliged. Or perhaps a better way of putting it is that it would be daft to miss the obvious opportunity, when it's relatively easy to do and the market is growing so fast. It's like not having an online presence – where once you could get away with it, now it's expected. You'd look odd / or not serious about what you're doing without it.

"I wanted to make my writing as accessible as possible to the widest audience"

- Linda

It seems there is a degree of obligation, but also recognition of opportunity. I always wanted to use the digital route, because I thought there were great advantages to the customer in terms of speed of delivery and also to the publisher in terms of cost of production. But I think that it is only now that the marketplace has begun to mature to the extent it has that it is possible to have success in this area. I also believe that electronic formats lend themselves better to some areas of writing than others, and also to some types of readers than others.

Of course there would be no ePublishing without readers of eBooks. Where do our authors fit in to this – have they embraced the digital book in their own lives?

What is your personal experience of reading electronic books?

Sallyann: I only read eBooks now since physically its difficult for me to hold and read a printed book for any time. I bought a Kindle almost two years ago and the number of books I read has increased enormously (and was already high compared to most readers). This is due in part to speed of purchase, ease of browsing, 24hr availability, less expensive books in the main and ultimately, for me, physical ease of reading.

Wendy: Quite good – surprisingly.

Simon: I've tried an experiment with it, and appreciate how easy and user friendly it is. But I still prefer books. I like the physical touch, and having shelves full of the things.

Linda: I was given a Kindle at Christmas 2010 as I was going to Australia for a long holiday. I like the way that I can annotate, easily pick up new books, reach the web and it's portable. However, I still love the smell and feel of a brand new book.

I am still a way behind our authors, as I have not yet embraced the digital book at all. I don't have an eReader and I hate reading books on the computer screen so I don't do it. For people like me, I believe there is always a reason to have a print version available – unless and until the balance tips so far that print becomes obsolete. I wonder if that will ever happen, or if it is a myth, like that of the paperless office.

Now we know where our authors are up to in their digital publishing and reading, I asked about their feelings regarding the progress in this area.

How do you feel about the rise of ePublishing in the last couple of years?

"It's just something which is now part of the publishing world which writers have to embrace"

- Simon

Simon: I don't have any particular feelings about it. It's just something which is now part of the publishing world which writers have to embrace. My real concern is that the industry clearly still doesn't quite know how to deal with it, and that marketing and business models which have worked for years are now having to be re-thought. That's tending to limit innovation and investment – taking risks – with new authors, which is unfortunate. But I think that will work itself out as it becomes clear exactly what ePublishing will mean.

Linda: I've embraced it myself. But I must admit that it does mean there are now no barriers to entry and much is released that isn't formatted correctly, with spelling and grammatical errors and very badly written.

Sallyann: At first, I kicked against it as I love the feel, smell and kinship with physical books. I still do. But this has allowed me to remain an avid reader and there are many others in my situation. I also note many people who use technology such as mobiles, laptops, eReaders etc., who were not book buyers or readers, do download and often read eBooks.

Now I see it as a valuable add-on where publishing is concerned. The downside is the quality of what's put out there. But any self-publishing could be said to do that so ultimately it's for readers to discern what they regard as a good read.

Wendy: I think it is daunting yet unstoppable.

Overall the feelings seem to be positive. Mine certainly are, in spite of my own foot-dragging as a reader. I recognise that not everyone is the same as me and am pleased to think that this will only be the beginning of what is to come.

On the other hand, there is some mention of the potential downside to this digital revolution, so let's look at that in more detail.

What concerns do you have about the lowering of 'barriers to entry' in publishing due to the ease and low costs of ePublishing?

Simon: None at all. There was always the print-on-demand / self-publishing market, which gave rise to concerns about quality being eroded. But readers aren't daft – they know where to find quality books, be it online or in more traditional formats. And if someone spends years writing a book, and then gets it published online and it makes them happy – and a few people read it – I can't see anything wrong with that.

Linda: Weeding out the dross becomes more difficult, but with experience it's easier to spot it. Poor cover design images, badly written blurbs etc.

Sallyann: I believe it's probably the same as self-publishing whereby the author is the final (often the only) arbiter of what's published. There are obvious pros and cons yet ultimately the readers decide. It's far less costly than self or conventional publishing so we're bound to have quantity over quality in some respects. Yet it's a subjective field and I trust also that many great books will reach an audience they otherwise wouldn't have.

Wendy: It can only be a good thing as it stops publishing being precious, but I can see you are going to have to sift out a lot of junk.

From our authors' perspective it seems that the lowering of barriers to entry due to ePublishing is just more of the same – a continuation of the progression which technological advances have caused in self-publishing. So perhaps the effects are not so new after all.

There are a couple of useful points contained here. Speaking as readers, our authors are recognising that there is a lot more 'chaff' to sort through to get to the 'wheat'. I suppose it's a bit like discovering Lord of the Rings (or whatever you consider a jewel of writing to be for you) buried amongst the 'slush pile' that probably still exists at every traditional publishing house. It's brilliant, it's there, but will you find it?

Now we all have access to pretty much the whole slush pile. Perhaps we will gain some respect for what those traditional publishers have tried to do in sifting that information for us. Certainly we will have to develop the skills to find that excellent writing for ourselves. Linda has given us some hints in red flags to be avoided – and as a writer you will certainly want to be sure you steer clear of these.

One way to attempt to get your writing noticed amongst the turmoil of words out there is to let people sample it without charging anything – by giving away your writing. But given how much free content is now available, will the whole world of paying for books come crashing down? What do our authors have to say on this subject?

Do you feel that the amount of free content now made available will affect the book market as a whole? What adverse effects do you envisage?

Linda: I don't envisage any adverse effects. Business and marketing has always worked well on the free model. I see it as an opportunity to find new talent. I've found

> "Business and marketing has always worked well on the free model"
> - Linda

As writers
it's up to us
to embrace
the concept
of free in
order to
reach new
readers

that I'm picking up books in genres I never would have touched before. If I like what they write then I will probably buy their next book.

Wendy: I see it as much greater advertising for my work for less cost to me. The adverse effect would be as before – sifting out the wheat from the chaff.

Sallyann: As with the arrival of computers, many people entered the world of desk top publishing initially without having any design flair or knowledge as to what worked or why. Ultimately the pendulum swung back to middle ground whilst also changing the face of marketing and design. What worked before and after stayed, in the main, and what didn't ultimately fell by the wayside!

Simon: I don't feel it will have a great impact. As I said above, readers know where to find quality work. Word of mouth is the key, and word soon gets around about whether something is worth reading or not. No one has to read a book. It takes but a few seconds of looking at a page or two to know if it's worth persevering with.

This is very interesting. Media hype surrounding the ePublishing revolution would have us believe that the whole edifice of publishing is about to crumble. That's not how our authors see things though, is it? Are they naïve, or overly optimistic? Or are they simply judging by their own behaviour and that of those they see around them?

My feeling is that there may be a downward pressure on prices, but perhaps this will be countered by people being able to purchase more books rather than less. I am heartened by the fact that my teenage son, although he has access to all the distractions and entertainments that new technology brings, still wants to pick up and escape into a book.

Linda has already said that having access to free content to try out new genres has broadened her reading. So it seems that as writers it's up to us to embrace the concept of free in order to reach new readers, incorporate it into our promotion, make sure we deliver the standard required and then reap the benefits! Well that's certainly something that I plan to do differently for future books, but how about our authors? Are they making any changes to their future plans?

What might you plan or do differently for future projects as a result of these changes?

> **Wendy:** Appreciate that I am not just writing for the traditional style of presentation and keep up to date with trends and formats.
>
> **Linda:** I'm not sure I'd change anything. I love both sides of the business as they appeal equally to different readers.
>
> **Sallyann:** I am definitely looking to publish more eBooks whilst still using conventional publishers for certain projects. The world is now truly our marketplace and I write books because I want to write a book (as opposed to wanting to have written a book). This ensures I do my best in honour of my readers. And, I trust, when we, as writers, work and write with this integrity, outcomes are favourable for all.
>
> **Simon:** Nothing! I write because I love it. The fact that people buy and read my scribblings is an added bonus.

"Books are no more threatened by Kindle than stairs by elevators"

- Stephen Fry

Technology is only ever a tool. How it affects us depends on our response and actions. Understanding the technology, and how it alters the behaviour of our readers is obviously vital. The truth is that the rise of ePublishing is a tremendous opportunity for writers. The barriers to entry are now all but gone, and it is true that marketing skills will be more necessary than ever. But all the information we need to make the most of this revolution is accessible. We can now try different strategies for little or no cost. I hope you feel as optimistic about the future of publishing as our authors obviously do.

"Publishing may be in trouble, but storytelling is not."

- Erica Wagner

7

The Process Of Writing

... in which we look at what is involved in writing a book and how our authors manage such a potentially daunting prospect.

"When I sit down at my writing desk, time seems to vanish. I think it's a wonderful way to spend one's life."

- Erica Jong

Most of us have some imagination – we need it to enjoy reading books.

There are a lot of preconceptions about what is needed to make a successful author, but ultimately it depends on your intended audience and the type of book you are trying to produce. Is it a literary tome for highbrow readers, or something to amuse or instruct? Each will need a different style.

So, setting aside what you might feel about the skills needed, let's get down to the nitty-gritty – the process of writing. Let's start by dealing with one belief that many people have – that you need a fabulous imagination to become an author.

Do you think you have a vivid imagination?

Simon: Yes, very much so. Ever since I was a kid, I've had imaginary friends. Many stay with me to this day. It's not uncommon for me to be travelling to a story for my day job and talking to my characters about how to cover it, or what might have motivated the crime.

Linda: Oh yes, but how much I use it depends on what I am writing. If it is self-help or how to books then I need to be able to project what questions the reader has and answer them. But that is the limit of the imagination needed. Fiction, of course, is completely different.

Wendy: Yes and no.

Sallyann: Not particularly, though I do find myself plotting story ideas in my head.

Our authors vary – some of them do have a strong imagination, others are not so sure. For myself, I would say that I'm about average. Most of us have some imagination – we need it to enjoy reading books. And I have yet to come across an author who does not *love* reading. Does your own level of imagination determine whether you will be able to write fiction or have to stick to non-fiction?

Do you need an imagination to write fiction?

Simon: Yes - it's the cornerstone of the art, but being a good observer of people and life can carry you a long way too.

Sallyann: I don't think so, because the sort of fiction I enjoy writing (and reading) is about contemporary life – almost like a social commentary about life today.

Linda: Definitely, though you can base fiction on your own life, so you might get away with changing places, characters and names.

Wendy: Not necessarily as you can draw from your own life and experience.

Opinion is divided here as well. Some feel you must be able to picture things vividly in order to create a believable fiction world. It seems to me that most fiction starts from a simple 'what if?' premise. For Simon, 'What if a TV crime reporter got involved in solving the crimes?' For Sallyann, 'What if an ordinary person was driven by circumstances to contemplate murder?' What is needed most seems to be curiosity and fascination, mostly with people.

Whether you decide to write fiction or non-fiction for your first book, you might be wondering how much you need to write.

How did you know how many words to write?

Wendy: I had decided that my book would be a small book – one that could be picked up and dipped into easily. Therefore I wanted to write a series of short books rather than one long book.

Linda: It depends on what I'm trying to say – sometimes less is more in a non-fiction book that is designed to give people enough information they can easily digest to make appropriate choices. Fiction is different; it depends on the audience and the subject. The average length of fiction is about 60,000 words and that's just about how long my novel is. It wasn't designed that way though.

Sallyann: I knew the rough length of a mainstream novel would be 80,000 words, but the story did just finish where it did, and it just happened to be close to that number. I would never pad a book out unless more explanation was needed – I do tend to write quite concisely, so I rarely have to cut a lot out.

Simon: I didn't. I just started writing a story. I think that's how you should begin - just give it a try. If it starts to work out, you can always cut or add words later.

Just because books are "usually" a certain length does not mean yours has to be.

This is one thing I have definitely learned from my association with other authors – not to get hooked on a pre-conceived notion. When I was writing my book I had researched average lengths of books in the field and was determined that mine would be a 'proper' book length. I had no trouble in making it that length as there was so much that I wanted to say, and I ended up with a book that covers all stages of the cancer journey from diagnosis onwards.

Having gone through the self-publishing route (where the costs of printing include a cost per page) this resulted in having to set the price at quite a high level. A different approach might have been to break the book down into a series of shorter books, which are relevant at different times and in different situations, allowing for a lower cover price. This might also have made the marketing more targeted.

There are also other considerations that affect the price (and length) of a book. How much content is needed to deliver the information you are offering? How much is the average cost of a book in the genre in which you are writing? The market is unlikely to stand a much higher than average price unless your book delivers something that is in very high demand. This may then in turn affect how much content you can include or the level of royalties you may have to accept.

ePublishing particularly lends itself to production of shorter 'bite-size' books or booklets – for instance there is now a strong market for individual short stories on Amazon Kindle where previously the only market would have been through magazines.

Just because books are 'usually' a certain length does not mean yours has to be – the difference may even make it stand out from the crowd. And certainly for non-fiction books some of the most successful are the shorter books, where you can get the information you need quickly and easily and it is faster to look up the pieces you need again.

Now we have dealt with the length of your book, what about your doubts and fears – will they stop you from making progress with your writing?

Did you have any self-doubt when writing your first book?

Wendy: No, I didn't have any doubt over writing the first book, but over time it has become more difficult to apply myself to writing because of procrastination.

Sallyann: As the first book was commissioned, I would not have taken it on if I didn't believe I could do it, so I didn't with that one. I'm not a prolific writer these days, and I only write what I strongly believe will be published. When self-doubt does creep in I use this belief to get myself back on track.

Linda: It depends - you are putting yourself on the firing line and raising your head above the parapet. I take it far more to heart when the tiny numbers of people criticise than the hundreds who praise. I didn't doubt my writing ability, though, as I'd been writing information on a website people already enjoyed.

Simon: Yes! And the second, and the third, and the fourth... and I know I always will, no matter how many I write. Don't be surprised by this. It's a human instinct. Anyone who doesn't suffer from it should be treated with great suspicion – it probably means either they're not human, or what they're writing is dung.

It seems to be a case of finding your own belief in yourself – or gritting your teeth and doing it anyway. I wasn't fearful during the process of writing my book, as it was so important to me to get it out there. I was afraid of going it alone though, which resulted in a lot of waiting and frustration whilst I was looking into the traditional publishing route. I had to be challenged to carry on writing in order to get past that, and that seemed to free me up to consider self-publishing.

I have now given up on self-doubt and decided to write whatever books interest me and I think might appeal to others. As long as I am able to let the right audience know about them, they will live their own lives.

Even if there is going to be some fear and doubt involved, this is normal. The next step, then, is to decide on your approach. Are you going to plan your writing in advance or just let it flow? What did our contributors do?

Did you plan your book, or write it as it came to you?

Wendy: I planned it by writing my chapter headings down first.

Linda: I was fortunate in that I already had a bank of email questions to work with which meant that my first book was already half planned. Most of the others were also planned as they were non-fiction and I knew I had to cover things logically. However my novel was completely different. That was literally 'stream of consciousness' writing and I never knew what was going to come out in the process of writing each day.

Simon: I planned it, and I'd recommend that. You should have some kind of narrative to follow, so you're always telling a story, be it a plot, a character's, or a mix.

Without a plan, it's all too easy to get lost. Tedious as it may sound, and change as it doubtless will, you've got to spend some time planning before you get to the fun bit of the actual writing.

Sallyann: With non-fiction I always did a chapter-by-chapter outline. For the novel the planning was more loose, but once I started writing it was as if the character took off in a different direction and the book had a different ending than I had expected. It's great to start with a plan, but be prepared to change it or even throw it out of the window.

Our authors seem to feel that planning is an important part of the process, though with fiction writing it may be optional. All writing must have a beginning, middle and a satisfying conclusion though (at least I think so; I hate books that end with no finale). It might be hard to start writing unless you have some idea what those might be, so how might you go about planning your book?

There are many different methods of planning. For those with a visual orientation, mind-mapping might be particularly appropriate. This can be done simply with a pen and paper or by using a mind-mapping software, which can be useful if you want to play with the structure and try moving parts from one place to another.

Alternatively for non-fiction you could brainstorm chapter titles then move them around into different structures until they make logical sense and a good progression through the book.

For my first book, I already had the structure of talking about a journey, so I made my chapters relate to stages of that journey. I listed the topics involved in each chapter, and even broke these down into subtopics. I then had a very detailed plan to work through, and each subtopic was only a few paragraphs of writing. For this book, on the other hand, a lot of the structure came from the questions I asked my contributors. I wrote them on post-it notes and organised them into groups that then became my chapters.

Let's check how our authors knew what to put into their books.

How do you decide what to put in a book and what to leave out?

> "Every word has to earn its living."
>
> - Sallyann

Wendy : Just by writing and editing it. Editing is the most important because it's like polishing a piece of furniture – you polish out all the debris from your writing.

Linda : That isn't a problem generally in non-fiction as I work with what I know the readers want. In fiction it's harder as it is so subjective.

Sallyann : Every word has to earn its living. Mainly I write everything as it comes, but then I go back over, revise and edit a lot. I concentrate on making sure the opening is compelling and that the story doesn't fall flat. Eventually though, you just have to draw a line under it and stop revising, and let it stand as it is.

With all the planning in the world, it is still possible to feel overwhelmed at the task ahead. How did our authors avoid or handle this issue?

How did you manage not to get overwhelmed at the size of the project of writing a book?

Sallyann: It didn't seem overwhelming to write my novel as I was just writing the story as it came out. I was enjoying the process of writing. Perhaps writing the non-fiction books before had helped because I already knew I could do it. With those books having a plan meant the task was broken down into chunks and so was more manageable.

Simon: By not thinking about it too much, and by loving the idea. And by seeing it as development by development in the book, rather than one great edifice. Confine yourself to thinking about what's happening next in the story, and it makes it far less daunting.

Wendy : I didn't give it any thought.

Linda: As I was working for myself, it was simply my job for the two months it took me to actually complete it. When I wrote my novel I took myself off to a cottage alone with no internet or telephone for a week at a time.

It seems that planning can help, as can not having too many expectations. Wendy says she didn't think about it, and I believe this is because she was enjoying the process. For me the planning was vital. Working without a publisher meant there was no deadline; the book would simply be finished when it was. For fiction books it is normal to complete the whole manuscript before approaching agents or publishers so again there is no deadline.

It is possible that you might want to set yourself a deadline, if you know from experience that this is the only way to get things done. I have found from my own experience, however, that writing develops its own momentum. The more you do, the more you want to write.

How might you manage your writing time – and find room for it in your life in the first place? How do our authors handle this?

How do you structure your writing time – in large blocks or small pieces?

Linda: I much prefer large blocks because I can concentrate – the problem is that a large block for me needs to be a month or two, rather than a day or two.

Sallyann: In large blocks, normally. I do a lot of writing in my head in between sitting at the computer. Once I start the book, the writing time isn't that long as I tend to become very absorbed and it almost takes over. I find the more I write the more I want to write and other things just fall by the wayside.

Simon: I don't think you can dictate when inspiration will strike. If it does, let it. If it doesn't, wait for it, but don't get frustrated. It'll come. You will, however, notice

> "I find the more I write the more I want to write and other things just fall by the wayside."
>
> - Sallyann

when you tend to do your best writing. With me, it's in the morning, when I'm fresh. Others write in the small hours. Just go with whatever works for you.

When I was writing my book I was a mother to two quite small children, and also spent quite a lot of time on my property administration day job. For me, the only way to write at all was in small pieces. This is where my planning paid off. Each section I had on my plan was only about two or three paragraphs, and the ideas were already in my head due to the planning process. I was able to write a section in only about half an hour – sometimes even less. For a long time I would write a section at my computer whilst eating my morning toast – then try to fit in another section later in the day. As I got further into the book I was snatching more of these half-hours and I felt very satisfied as I saw my chart of what I had written fill up.

The amount of time you have to write will vary depending on what else is going on in your life, but it is something you are doing for yourself. Everyone should be able to find a little time in life for themselves. Are our authors able to give us any more insights into finding time?

How much time would you spend writing in a typical week when working on your first book, and how did you find that time?

Simon: I try to do a couple of hours a day, but always give myself one day off a week to recharge. I think that's a good idea, we all need a break. Some days you can do more, others less. Don't be dogmatic about what time you have to spend - that's a sure way to scare off inspiration. Just feel it and go with it - almost let the book write itself through you.

Linda: It was a full time job for me.

You may think that Linda is unusual in being able to make writing a full-time job, but in fact this has been the case for quite a few authors. Some take a sabbatical from work, just as you might if you wanted to travel around the world. Of course you might want to save up some funds first. Author Lee Child got started when he was made redundant from his job and decided that rather than looking for another he would make a living from writing. Was he naïve? Possibly, but that belief and the determination that it had to work seem to have done the trick for him. Would his approach still work in today's publishing world? Who knows? It's not an approach I would personally advise unless you have another source of income and/or an extremely understanding partner. On the other hand, if you find yourself out of work or retired, what harm is there in using at least some of your time in this way?

> "I want to be a best-selling author, not a best-writing author!"
>
> - Robert Kiyosaki

Another fear that may come up during writing is that of 'worthiness'. How do you as a writer know that you can attain a suitable standard? The perception used to be that agents and publishers were the gatekeepers. They determined what standards of writing should be adhered to. However the truth is that there has always been a lot of luck involved – as can be seen from the fact that so many extremely successful books were rejected time and time again before they got their chance. Now, with the rise of print-on-demand, anyone can print whatever book they like – and instead we have feedback from the marketplace, with readers reviews holding much more weight in assessing the quality of the book. But you can't get that feedback until the book is out there, and we have already seen that it is hard to handle negative feedback when we looked at self-doubt earlier in this chapter (I'm no stranger to this myself). How can you handle this particular fear?

How did you know you could write well enough to be published?

Simon: I didn't and you won't - that's for the readers out there to decide, amongst them agents, publishers and editors.

Linda: I didn't, but I did have a loyal following on the website who commented on the information that was there and as I'd written all that content myself, it was a reasonably easy assumption to make that I could replicate it in a book.

Sallyann: Because I was already working in a writing profession, my background gave me that confidence. When you're self-employed as I was you only continue to get work if you are doing a good job. Some of my clients were publishers, too!

Unless you are a professional writer already, the chances are you won't know how well you can write. You could choose the long road and gain that experience as Sallyann did. Write short pieces for magazines and newspapers and keep submitting them until you get something published. Enter writing competitions. You could join a local writers group and gain experience that way. You could offer to write theatre reviews for your local newspaper, as Wendy has done. The chances are you will be paid little or nothing, but you will be practising your craft.

You can also gain some knowledge from books, but most writers say the best way to get better at writing is to write – and indeed if you compare early and later books from many authors you will see a considerable difference in skill. It's important though to remember that the quality of the message matters most. There are awards for the best-written books, and receiving them is fantastic for the authors concerned. But the best reward of all is from people choosing to buy your book. Robert Kiyosaki (author of the Rich Dad series of books) says 'I want to be a best-selling author, not a best-writing author!'

You can, of course, also employ a professional editor to look over your work. This is something I did for my first book and it did make a difference – I knew I had done what I could to make the book as professional as possible. There are even services which will (for a fee) look over your manuscript and comment on the quality for you. These may be worthwhile to give you confidence in your early days, but the best feedback you are likely to get is from people who are in the target audience for your book, as long as they are able to be honest with you.

This means it may not be the people who are closest to you who are the best ones to ask for feedback. They may be biased, or fearful of your reaction if they are honest. Also, if they are critical it could be difficult for you emotionally. Experience makes a difference here as well. I have found that over time I am less attached to the exact words I write, and happier to receive feedback through which I can improve the end result.

Assuming you can find some time to write and get past any worries about the quality of your writing, there is still the challenge of the size of the project. Some books are small and can be completed quickly – others take a long time. Personalities also vary. Some people are great at having ideas and starting projects, but then find it hard to complete them. How did our authors manage to make sure they stuck with the program long enough to finish their books?

How did you find enough commitment to complete your first book?

> **Simon:** By believing in it, as outlined above. I can't emphasise enough - belief is the key. It can carry you just about anywhere.
>
> **Sallyann:** The nearer I get to the end, the more incentive I have to finish. It's that thing of seeing the finishing tape.
>
> **Linda:** I needed to get enough money together to pay the bills, that is a great motivator.

I had a combination of Simon and Sallyann's motivators. I believed so strongly in the book that it never occurred to me at any point to stop. I also found the momentum building as I worked through my plan. I am a person who likes ticking items off a list, so for me having a chart of my book chapters and subsections up on the wall and filling in the ones I had written made a big difference. Seeing the amount of white space gradually going down was very satisfying indeed, and there was no way that I wasn't going to finish.

Not everyone is so fortunate, though. Some writers experience blocks along the way and have to find ways around them.

Did you ever get stuck whilst writing, and if so how did you get past that?

Wendy: I got stuck in the second book and I got through it by leaving it for a little while, or showing it to someone and bouncing ideas off them which enabled me to get unstuck.

Simon: Yes, and all writers sometimes do. The worst thing you can do is let it wind you up and find yourself getting frustrated. That's no way to write. It's a hard lesson to learn, but take it from me - the best thing to do when stuck is walk away. What seems impossible now, will feel straightforward later. I promise!

Linda: I can't say I did with the first, but with my sixth which is fiction – that was a completely different matter entirely. In the end I went away for a week to somewhere completely different with my laptop. I came back realising that what I had thought was the beginning of a novel was just a short story and with 40,000 words of a completely different novel already written.

It might help to be aware that one reason for getting stuck might be either not knowing what you will do when the book is finished, or even fear of what you will have to do next (i.e. show it to someone else, laying yourself open to the possibility of rejection).

Hopefully this book will give you a clearer picture of where you are going, and show that you can take that next step as others have before.

What kept you going if you had doubts about success?

Simon: Belief again. Bloodymindedness helps too, but mainly belief.

Sallyann: I did have to leave the novel for a while as I found the emotions I was writing about so raw. Then ultimately I just had to sit at the computer and make myself do it. I said to myself, "If you want to be a novelist then you have to finish your novel!"

Linda: The knowledge that I already had a ready-made audience for the non-fiction. The fiction was more 'suck it and see' and a story that had to be written to satisfy that 'itch' I had.

Wendy: People asking when the next book was coming out! In the end I decided that I just had to get on and finish it.

It really can be as simple as Wendy says – just making a decision to get on with it. In fact Wendy's second book, *Get Cracking*, is a great motivator to do just that!

One thing that new authors are sometimes recommended to do is to collaborate on a book project with someone else who is perhaps better known than them. I have had this suggested to me on several occasions. One of our authors has experience of collaborating on a book, so what can she tell us about the process?

What is your experience of collaboration on a book project – is it something you would recommend to other authors?

Wendy: I collaborated with my artist. In the beginning it was very exciting and the collaboration definitely enhanced my book. Then the artist began to take too much interest in the written work beyond what I felt was reasonable. I would recommend other authors not to be too sensitive about the other person's input about your work – stick to your guns!

I personally have resisted the suggestion to collaborate in the past. I felt that those who are high-profile as suggested were not necessarily in tune with the approach in my book, so why would they want to collaborate with me, or I with them? Perhaps I am holding myself back by this attitude. It is certainly true to say that there are some definite pitfalls to collaboration.

It is like a business partnership – and you can draw some parallels from that.

Often people go into partnership based on trust alone without drawing up any clear guidelines as to how the relationship will work. The assumption seems to be that the personal relationship between the people will handle any issues, and that being too formal is somehow disloyal to the friendship. There are times when this approach works, and others where it leads to disaster! If you are collaborating, I suggest drawing up a clear list as to what input is required from all concerned – and how the revenues will be split.

For this book, although I have contributions from other authors, it is not a true collaboration. I am in control of the whole project; the final content of the book is determined by me. The authors answered my questions, we had an agreement that I could use their words and the rest of it was up to me.

As you go ahead with your writing project, how long is it realistic to envisage that the process will take?

How long did it take you to write your book from start to finish?

> **Simon:** First draft, 3 months. But that's just the start. Then 6 rewrites - in total, one year approx. I think that feels about right.
>
> **Linda:** About four months altogether.
>
> **Sallyann:** My first book was 3 months from start to first draft. My first novel was about 18 months from conception to being ready to send to the publishers.

It can vary from book to book, and depends on how much time you have available. For me it was a year and three months from getting clarity on the idea of the book to having it in print. Of course the writing is just the beginning, as we shall be covering in the chapter on **Getting The Word Out**.

Allowing three years for word of mouth to take full effect, plus up to two years to write your book in the first place, it seems you need to expect to be involved with your book for at least five years. If you believe in your book, living with it and being passionate about it for that length of time will not be a problem.

It may also depend on what your reason is for writing. Are you writing a book to raise your profile? In that case it is part of the marketing you would be doing anyway. Do you have a burning desire to top the bestseller lists? Or do you simply want to have written a book? Nobody can tell you that your motivation is wrong, but only you can know if it is strong enough to see you through.

"Write while the heat is in you. The writer who postpones the recording of his thoughts uses an iron which has cooled to burn a hole with. He cannot inflame the minds of his audience."

- Henry David Thoreau

8

Self-Fulfilment

... in which we discover what the completion of
a writing project means to our authors

"Happiness lies in the joy of achievement and the thrill of creative effort."

- Franklin D. Roosevelt

Having looked at some of the issues that might come up while you are writing your book, let's move on to the positives. You've already seen that writing a book can be quite an undertaking, that you need to be prepared to put in your energy and your passion and that there will be obstacles to overcome. What about the other side of the coin?

There are many thousands of books published every year, many of them by new authors. They would not put in all that work unless they were getting something out of the process – or they expected there to be some reward.

What are the pluses of writing in terms of internal benefits? When might they materialise? Do the authors change as they write or do those benefits come later? Let's start by finding out how they thought about themselves whilst writing their first book.

Could you picture yourself as an author whilst writing your first book?

Simon: No. Just someone trying out a new hobby, and I think that's a healthy thing to do.

Sallyann: Yes, I was very excited about that. When starting on fiction it was harder to think of myself as a novelist. I'm still working on that one.

Linda: I don't think I'd ever thought about it. It only dawned on me this year (in 2012) and after seven books over seven years that I was in fact an author.

Wendy: No. In the beginning I was just a writer, now people refer to me as an author and I'm getting more used to it!

For Sallyann, it seems that it was a development as she had already been writing for some time. Perhaps she was ready to think of herself that way. For me, like the other authors, I didn't really feel any different about myself. Mostly I was relieved that after many years I finally knew what to write. I had no doubt that I would finish the book because of my passion for the subject, but I could not really picture what would come next.

I think the key to self-fulfilment as an author is not to look too far ahead. It's important to enjoy the process of writing for its own sake. If you don't, if it feels like a chore or a job, then that doesn't mean you should not continue to write. But the reasons for doing it will be different. For most people who have a desire to write, they will enjoy the process. There is a huge satisfaction in crafting words that will mean something to another person.

> There is a huge satisfaction in crafting words that will mean something to another person.

In every author's life there is one extra-special moment – that of holding the first copy of your first book! Our authors share how that felt for them.

How did it feel when you first held a copy of your book?

Simon: Amazing. I took it everywhere with me. It feels like all the work is finally worth it. I don't have kids, but I've heard other authors describe it as like having a new baby. You keep looking at it and don't want to be parted from it.

Sallyann: Amazing!

Linda: A bit nervous of making it available in case people didn't like it.

For me it was like Simon and Sallyann – I loved holding my book. I thought it was beautiful! I was so pleased with the cover, and amazed after so long that it was really done. It was very much 'my baby' and thankfully my husband also shared some of my enthusiasm (perhaps because of all the work he had done editing, formatting and indexing the book).

Please be aware, though, that not everyone will necessarily share your enthusiasm. One author I met told of her mother's response when first shown her book. "Well, I thought it would have been in hardcover" was the disparaging comment. You may sometimes have to be proud for yourself, and accept that your book will not be for everyone.

Looking back, what differences have writing made in the lives of our authors? Did it help them grow as a person?

What did publishing your book mean to you in terms of self-fulfilment or growth?

Sallyann: To have crafted the novel gave me a lot of personal fulfilment. As I have also taught creative writing it showed that I was standing up for what I was teaching – putting my money where my mouth was if you like. I wanted to write something I would be happy to read.

Linda: It's something to add to my CV, it has increased my profile significantly and it portrays me as an expert (which I may not be). I have more confidence as people regularly tell me how helpful the books have been, and of course I'm earning a decent living from my creative endeavours which is hugely satisfying.

Simon: It certainly gives you a sense of achievement and self worth. It feels as though you've done something which will last, a legacy almost, albeit a small one.

Wendy: It was a definite growth and progress in my self-fulfilment. I learnt a lot about myself, about the discipline of writing and about producing something from start to finish.

Make no mistake; writing a book from start to finish is a huge achievement. Many more have the idea than ever make a serious start on the project. And a large percentage of those who start do not make it to the finishing line. You are absolutely bound to grow in the process. I know I did. One of the great things about a book is that it is a concrete reminder of your achievement. It can never be 'unwritten'. It may also give you the confidence to tackle other projects in your life.

Getting it out into the world will almost certainly lead to experiences you have never envisaged.

What is the best thing that has happened to you as a result of writing your book?

Wendy: I wrote another! I'm now living my dream to be a writer. It's opened doors and I now write reviews for the local paper as well.

Sallyann: The amount of positive feedback has been fabulous. There is also a lifestyle it gives you of being able to meet interesting people. I really enjoy the signings and meeting new people.

Linda: The recognition I get as an author. I'm invited to speak at conferences; other authors refer to my books in their books; and I get lots of emails from people telling me they loved my books.

Simon: I've discovered a new life. One of doing talks to readers at libraries, and literary festivals. One of feeling very appreciated, when you get emails from people telling you how much they love your work. It's a new world, and a wonderful one.

"It's a new world and a wonderful one."

- Simon

For me the best thing so far has been having someone come up to me and say that my book quite literally changed her life. This lady was at her wits end with a family member's cancer, with feelings in turmoil. She felt that my writing gave her permission to have whatever feelings she did without having to feel guilty about them. My message had truly landed with someone it was destined for.

What about your book? What's the best thing that could happen to you as a result of it? Why not think about that now and make some notes? It could be picturing your ideal 'day as an author' or writing a review of your book from someone who has appreciated it in the way you intended.

"When I'm writing, I know I'm doing the thing I was born to do."

- Anne Sexton

9

Getting The Word Out

... in which we consider what is involved in
promoting a book in today's world

> "To write something, you have to risk making a fool of yourself."

> - Anne Rice

Authors love to write. This usually involves sitting by themselves. Once upon a time it would have been with a pen and paper, then usually a typewriter. These days it will almost certainly be you and your computer. And this is where it could end if you want. If you are simply writing for personal satisfaction you could leave your work on the electronic page and do nothing more with it. What a shame that would be.

Most people, whatever their fear and trepidation, can only fulfil their goals or intentions by making their book available to other people. This means that you are going to have to let people know that your book exists, and do so in a way that makes them feel they want to spend their money – and their time in order to read it.

Let's be clear at the outset. Getting the word out can feel like a different set of skills to writing. Some writers already have the skills and temperament which suit them to letting people know about their books. Others don't, but discover they have a flair for it. Still others never quite feel at ease, but find the ways that best suit their personality.

Book promotion has changed dramatically with the arrival of the Internet, and it's here that I start with our contributing authors:

You have used the Internet to spread the word about your books – do you think this is essential today, or is it still possible to get a book known without a computer?

Linda: No, not in today's hyper connected world. You have to be visible online. Even if you are traditionally published, your publishers will expect you to be on Facebook, Twitter, Goodreads and probably have a blog or website you update as well.

Simon: I think it's essential. It's the first place people now go to look you up so you need to be there. If you're not – people will ask why? Get a website and reserve your name as soon as you can. It's a powerful marketing tool and is expected.

Wendy: I think it is essential.

Sallyann: I think it makes things much easier because you can direct people to a website. You can promote locally without using a computer, but it is much harder to have a greater reach. Now it is possible to widen the market globally, which is fabulous for any author.

My view is that it depends on the purpose of your book. If your only intention is, say, to raise some money for a local charitable cause by selling a relevant book, then local marketing *might* be all that you need. But if the book has a larger potential audience, or they are more widely spread, or your local cause could benefit from more exposure, then the Internet is the way to reach much greater numbers of people – even those who live locally.

So how *does* the Internet help?

How do you think the Internet has helped you?

Linda: Most of my books are not the sort to be stocked by a bookshop, therefore it is the only way to sell them. The social networks help me to spread the world and talk to potential readers.

Simon: It helped spread the word of the books. There are lots of specialist crime fiction sites which are happy to review books and do interviews with up and coming authors. Target those (in whatever genre you write – because they are there) and you can start to make a name.

Sallyann: I have a website which helps with drawing feedback, and I have also been able to list my books on Amazon worldwide.

"Now it is possible to widen the market globally, which is fabulous for any author."

-

Sallyann

For myself, I think the Internet has helped by making available promotional channels that I am comfortable with and which are inexpensive. I created a website and a blog to back up the content of my first book, and was able to communicate with a worldwide audience. Though I have little time now to devote to that website, what I created is still there and still visible. Due to the nature of the book being not suitable for bookshops, without the Internet I really have no idea how I would have got the word out. Now I also have a job which takes up a lot of my time, so I am looking to the Internet to allow me to interact with people far and near in the relatively small amount of time I have available.

New authors are sometimes asked whether they have an 'author platform'. What does that mean, and how would you go about building one?

> **Linda:** For me it is about having a ready made audience that you can sell the book to. I was fortunate enough to have started The Hysterectomy Association in the mid 1990's which gave me my platform and my validity as an author in this field. With later business books it meant having a blog, being on social networks, speaking at business events and contributing to other business websites.
>
> **Simon:** I think it means whether you already have some recognition. To get a platform, you have to do the work I wrote about above - get out and sell yourself. Get your book in independent bookstores, do library talks, media interviews etc. Anything that helps get you known. And keep building the platform.
>
> **Sallyann:** Publishers can expect you to be known already. In non-fiction they like you to have experience in the field. If you write in your area of expertise you can get something out there and this helps you to build on your credentials.

As we talked about in the section on **Traditional Publishing vs Self-publishing**, the business of publishing involves risk – large amounts of it. Looking for authors who have a platform is one way that publishers reduce that risk. When I learned that a publisher would look for a platform – which just means having a strong group of people who know who you are and are interested in what you do – I thought there was nothing I could do to create one. Now I realise that if I had started my website and blog when I began writing my book (instead of doing it after publication), I would have been building that platform for myself and made the job of promoting the book much easier.

One thing that may make the task of promotion seem harder is the fact that there are other books out there. A completely new topic is a very rare thing, though there are always new angles and approaches. Do you need to worry about how your book compares to others in the field?

There are other people writing in the same genre as you – did you have to do anything to differentiate your books? Do you ever worry about the competition?

Sallyann: I never worry about competition as I believe there is enough for everybody. You could give a thousand people the same idea for a story and they would all write a different book! When I see other people being published then I feel joyful about that, as I think it just raises the profile of all authors.

Wendy: Yes – I differentiated by making mine in bite-size pieces. I don't worry about competition because there have always been books about personal development.

Linda: There wasn't competition for my first, second and third books and seven years on there still isn't. Although there are books about hysterectomy, they are very dry and factual whereas mine are highly practical and light hearted, which helps release the tension. There is more competition with the business books but taking a different approach helps. The novel is different again –

> "I never worry about competition as I believe there is enough for everybody."
>
> - Sallyann

there are huge numbers of other fiction books people can choose from, so making yours stand out is very difficult.

Simon: I think a unique angle helps. People seem to like the TV reporter/detective in my books. Some say everything's been done in writing, but that's nonsense. Life has infinite varieties, and it's a writer's job to mirror that. You can always find a new idea in a plot, or a new quirk to a character. I don't worry about the competition because I mainly write for myself. I'm just lucky - and delighted - that others like it too. If you need to do some research, my advice would be to go to a bookstore and get an idea of where there might be gaps in the market for something different.

I also do not really believe in competition. I think in non-fiction people researching a particular topic will very rarely buy only one book. Fiction readers will buy or read one book after another. In fact comparisons with other authors can be very helpful to you. Do you think it would help your sales if you were described as 'the next John Grisham' for instance?

A fresh approach is always helpful, though, as Linda says. In order for your non-fiction book to be chosen in addition to others in the field, it must add something that they don't. For a fiction book, there must be some particular appeal – an interesting character or a kind of plot that is unique. What you want is to hook people on your approach so they want to read other books from you.

What are the kinds of activities that you need to do in order to spread the word about your book?

How did you and your publisher get your book(s) known? How much is your responsibility, or is it up to you what you do in addition to the publisher's publicity?

Simon: It's a team effort. They'll support you, but you have to do the talks and interviews yourself. Do anything that's on offer when you're starting up. Anything that helps give you a profile. You should make contacts with librarians, literary festivals and journalists in your area. Ask the publishers to get in contact with such people in other areas, along with websites, trade journals, anything!

Wendy: I took my book to workshops, local bookshops, contacted local press, talked to groups and just always had a copy with me to show to anyone I met. Even if you do have a publisher you can't rely on what they do – ultimately your book is most important to you. Start with local bookshops. Make sure you have a poster they can display. Visit them in person and build a relationship.

Sallyann: The more any author can do off their own bat gives them an advantage. My publisher deals with the marketing but I would never sit back and expect them to uncover every opportunity. I still contact the media, but I consult with the publishers to make sure I'm on track. I do book signings, talks and competitions to win copies. I also look for links and associations within the novel to places or organisations to see if there are opportunities. I also get in touch with bookshops and offer to sign copies to give a greater prominence.

Linda: I got mine known through the website mostly, as I already had visitors there. From there it was easier to take it onto Amazon. The business books were helped by the amount of business networking I do.

> "Even if you do have a publisher you can't rely on what they do – ultimately your book is most important to you."
>
> - Wendy

Although it seems as though Linda didn't have to do anything to promote her book, this really hides the truth. She had just done the work already getting the website and The Hysterectomy Association known – through newspapers and magazines, using her computer and search engine knowledge and skills, and most of all through the women she helped spreading the word to others. I know that this is not as easy as it looks, as mine has been a work in progress for several years now, but gradually you can acquire those skills.

Even if you are working with a publisher, you should take care of your own Internet presence. Remember that as a business they are promoting many books, not just yours. You are the only one who can take charge of your own persona on the web, and this will give you the flexibility to publish in other ways in the future or use a different publisher if you want to write a different type of book or you are not happy with the relationship.

The Internet can seem like a relatively safe place – after all you are still just sat at home with your computer, maybe even in your pyjamas as I am whilst I'm writing this. In contrast, talking to bookshops or libraries can seem extremely daunting. There are ways to manage any fear you have, but ultimately the only way to reduce it is to do what you are afraid of. You may never lose the fear, but when a bookshop says "Yes, we will take your book" or a group says "Please come and talk to us" it will reinforce that there is a reason to what you are doing. Your book deserves the best you can give it, so get out there and spread the word.

And when do you start spreading the word?

When did your book promotion start related to the publication date?

Simon: A few weeks before - too soon, and you risk people forgetting, or having nothing to offer them in a short space of time in terms of the book. Too late and you miss an opportunity. People like things that are "new" - and journalists in particular do.

Linda: It started with an offer in Woman magazine who were doing an article on hysterectomy and had worked with me to find their case study ladies. It was in the same month as *101 Handy Hints for a Happy Hysterectomy* was published and resulted in a lot of awareness and a lot of sales. With my LinkedIn book I had already tried an experiment in social media the year before with a simpler pdf version. The paperback took off from there.

Sallyann: It's a delicate balance, as you have to make sure the book is available before you do too much work. If the book is available to pre-order that can help, but it can be frustrating for people to wait. You have to do a lot when the book is new but starting too soon can be counter-productive.

There seems to be an agreement here that promoting a book is best done when the book is available, or will be soon. There are a few exceptions to this. Very well-known authors like Richard Paul Evans who have a strong following of fans can announce a book publication date months in advance, and many people will pre-order it (books can be set up on Amazon with a future publication date). For future books you should also have a way to let readers of your previous books know about the new one – how will you keep in touch with them in order to do that? You may want to utilise social media such as Facebook or Twitter.

Also, bear in mind that even if your book is not ready, you can be promoting yourself and your ideas in some of the ways we've covered already – building that platform from which to launch yourself and your writing career to much greater heights. What are you waiting for?

"Understand that you need to sell you and your ideas in order to advance your career, gain more respect, and increase your success, influence and income."

- Jay Abraham

10

As Time Goes By

... in which we find out how life as an author
may change with the passage of time

"Time flies. It's up to you to be the navigator."

- Robert Orben

It's amazing what you can get used to. Before writing your first book, it seems such a big thing – shall I or shan't I? Can I write well enough? Will I be successful? Do I have what it takes? Once done, though, it doesn't end there. Life as an author stretches out ahead of you. You will always have written that book, and perhaps you will go on to write many more. What might the future hold for you? If you go on to write a string of books, how might the experience change? Will you still enjoy the process as much? Will the hopes and fears be different the second time around?

How did writing a second or subsequent book differ from the first one?

Simon: It felt as though there was more pressure. Because it had been commissioned, it meant I was writing against a deadline, which wasn't the case with the first. I also think I felt I had more to live up to, and that it had to be good, because I knew it would get published. That combination probably made for a worse book, but that's a common problem - it's known as "second book syndrome", and it's a curse of the trade.

Sallyann: For non-fiction it was much the same, and always just as exciting holding the first copy in your hand. The novel went up another level – it was like my defining moment. With writing the second novel there has been a bit of competition for time with promoting the first one, but the process of writing has been quite similar.

Wendy: It was more difficult. The expectation was quite high, but also there was more distraction. There was a little too much input from my collaborating artist.

Linda: Different subjects, different styles, different audiences - just a different experience altogether but still very much approached as my full time job.

So writing a second book can be a totally different experience. For a start you know what happened with the first book. You know what you had to do and what response you got. Your goals and expectations for subsequent books are likely to be different. For me, I think in some ways I left it too long before writing a second book – but I suppose I was taking the same approach as the first time. I couldn't get started until I knew who the book was for. I am unusual in writing a completely different second book – for a different audience. I'm not building on an existing fan base, and promoting this book will be just like starting from scratch again.

It is certainly true that there are more distractions the second time around. I now have a website to maintain, and promotion for the first book to continue taking care of, as well as my day job, but I am also immensely glad to be back to writing. Though I've written for the blog and the website, there is a different feeling to crafting a book. Building and honing it from the first idea to a finished product.

So if you are working on your first book, I suggest you enjoy the process. It will never feel quite like this again.

Of course you are not writing just for the pleasure of it – you have an idea of how you want your writing to affect your life. How do our authors feel about how things have turned out for them?

How do you feel about your life as an author and the income you get?

Wendy: I feel great about my life and my future as an author. Although financial rewards are slow to materialise I feel confident about this building in the future. The growth would be worth it even so.

> "I feel great about my life and my future as an author."
>
> - Wendy

Linda: Pretty satisfied if the truth be told. Getting monthly credits to my bank account from multiple sources is pretty satisfying.

Sallyann: I've been self-employed for a long time, so I'm used to ups and downs in my income – which is still the case. I do love the lifestyle it brings; you can't measure the joy financially. They say that if you do the work you love you'll never work a day in your life, and I can't imagine doing anything else now.

Simon: I don't worry about the money, as I still work full time for the BBC, and see writing as a hobby, but it is a lovely surprise to get the occasional cheque for royalties, PLR [Public Lending Rights – payments for books borrowed from libraries] or appearing at a festival. Regarding life as an author, I love it - for the simple reason that people tell me they enjoy the books, and that's more than enough. The ability to make someone's life a little happier is a decent part of the definition of a worthwhile existence, in my view.

In my case, I have had to accept that the financial rewards are slow to materialise. It can be important to be realistic about that. You don't make a lot from any one book, so you have to sell a lot of them if they are to provide your income. And I really mean *a lot*. The majority of books produced sell fewer than a hundred copies in their lifetime (source: Nielsen 2004), which is not going to put you firmly in the lap of luxury. But with persistence, if you keep writing and build up a following, if you have the time to allow your books to grow in popularity – then there is a lifestyle you can create. Our authors love that lifestyle, and it is within your grasp too.

What percentage of time do you now spend on promoting your books as opposed to writing?

Sallyann: I've been doing more promotion since the novel was published and less writing, and now it's swinging back the other way as I'm focusing on the next book. But I'll never stop the marketing completely and it takes up time following leads and trails to opportunities.

Linda: Roughly 50/50.

Simon: It's probably about half and half now. That feels about right - a mix of writing the things, and then talking about them.

I think half and half is just about perfect, too. Never give up on promoting a book you wrote. You poured your love and your craft into it; it deserves your continued attention. At the same time, one book on its own is rarely enough to create an author's life. So working on the next book and the next is important. You know yourself that if you discover an author and love the first book of theirs you read, your next step is likely to be to look what else they have written. Don't let your fans be disappointed for too long!

If you don't have the inspiration for the next book, by all means concentrate on promotion for a little while, but play with ideas in the meantime until inspiration does arrive. It's easy to get caught up in promotion and forget just how much you enjoy writing (I know because this is what I did!) If you have both writing and promotion in your life you are likely to feel more contented.

The life of an author does throw up unexpected twists and turns. I wondered what surprising or unusual experiences our authors had as a result of writing their books.

What is the oddest or most amusing thing that has happened?

Simon: I keep getting emails from people, complaining when my characters misbehave, or when I do something nasty or unpleasant in a book. I got one from a woman saying that Dan (the reporter/central character) is cruel to his dog because he keeps getting called out to stories at all hours, and leaves the poor creature alone for far too long. It's an example of how real the books can become to readers. And that's a good sign, however odd - it means you're writing convincingly.

Wendy: The oddest thing has been that I get more sales from a local café than from many bookshops. The most amusing is that I once sold five copies of my book at a funeral – it's called *Never Die Wondering*!

Linda: Being able to say to people that I wrote *101 Handy Hints for a Happy Hysterectomy* – they think it's a joke.

Sallyann: I got invited to a Christmas Fair of a hospital because I set one of my scenes in their waiting room. I was sat in the foyer signing books, which I could never have imagined when I was writing the book.

One thing is certain; you will be surprised at whose life your book will touch. It will reach places and people you could never have anticipated. And you will become a subtly different person – someone who has completed a project that many desire but do not manage. Will it affect how others see you?

Are you regarded any differently now that you are an author?

Sallyann: I'd like to think not – it's just what I do. It's been a long time now, so perhaps I'm not really aware of it. I've been in the business of writing for so long that everyone knows what I do.

Linda: I think I get an extra look of respect when I tell people I've written seven books of which three are bestsellers.

Simon: I think so. People are aware how tough it is to get published. Doing so certainly bestows extra respect.

I'm with Simon; I think I am regarded differently if people know about my book. Of course I have had to get used to telling people about it in order for that to happen. The people least likely to regard you differently are those closest to you.

"People are aware how tough it is to get published. Doing so certainly bestows extra respect."

- Simon

They're more likely to have the response of "oh, it's just another one of Anne's projects" or "I don't know what she's thinking – she'll never be the next JK Rowling!" On the other hand, people who don't know you will look at you differently than they would have otherwise. They will find you more interesting for one thing. Practice saying it. When people ask "What do you do?" say "I'm an author". You will be treated differently, and you may well find you like it.

"Time has been transformed, and we have changed; it has advanced and set us in motion; it has unveiled its face, inspiring us with bewilderment and exhilaration."

- Kahlil Gibran

11

Passing On Advice

... in which we ask our authors for any advice
they have with the benefit of hindsight.

"Many receive advice. Only the wise profit from it."

- Pubilius Syrus

This book has given you an opportunity – to step into the future and see how things could be for you if you choose writing as your path for the years ahead. Our contributing authors have been generous in giving their insights to help you on the way. Here is one last chapter where they speak to you directly. Firstly, they reflect on their own experiences:

With the benefit of hindsight, is there anything you would do differently in your writing career?

Simon: I'd have started it sooner. It's such a delight; I find it difficult to imagine what I did with much of my life before I started writing.

Linda: Yes, I'd stop adding in extra jobs to do and work full time as an author.

Wendy: Yes – much better allocation of time to write.

Sallyann: I sometimes think I would have written a novel sooner, but I also recognise it would have been a completely different book if I had. I am a bit reticent on the promotion and having a consistent marketing plan would have been a better approach. It does mean overcoming the emotional attachment and feeling of rejection, though.

For myself, I would go straight for the self-publishing option and worry less about what might be involved in that. I would also build up more slowly without investing so much money. Also I wish I had carried on to write a second book sooner, now that I remember how enjoyable it is!

So what further advice do our authors have for you?

Is there any particular advice you would like to pass on to others who would like to write?

Wendy: Just write! Don't question your ability, and leave editing till later – just write.

Simon: Just do it. Don't get hung up on whether you can, whether you're good enough, if your idea will work, whether you've got the time or commitment - just try. You never know until you do where it might all lead. Just look at what happened to me.

Sallyann: I think perseverance is the key. If you stick at it, are committed to improving and making the work the best you can, then ultimately you will be published. Only send your work out when it is the absolutely the best you can make it.

When you get feedback about your writing look at it setting aside your personal attachment. You might agree with them or not, but consider whether you have something to learn from their experience.

Linda: If it's in you, just get on and do it.

I think you might be detecting a theme here. If you want to write, you will gain from writing (you can only imagine what you might gain before you do it) and it's time to write now. If you're having trouble motivating yourself, or you are still held back in any way by fear, then I would recommend reading Wendy Knee's first two books *Never Die Wondering* and *Get Cracking*. Then write, write, write!

Don't worry about what you don't know – this will resolve itself as you go along. There is a saying – "when the student is ready, the teacher appears." Well, I suspect you are ready now. And here our authors share some of their favourite teachers:

> "Just write! Don't question your ability, and leave editing till later – just write."
>
> - Wendy

Are there any writers' resources you would especially recommend?

> "Some people like my advice so much that they frame it on the wall instead of using it."
>
> - Gordon R. Dickinson

Wendy: Join a writing group, use writing forums and read magazines. (eg Writer's Forum)

Sallyann: *Solutions for Writers* by Sol Stein. If you're serious about being a good writer (a book will never be rejected because it's too well written!!!) It's not the best first book if you have no expertise, but if you are interested in crafting and writing well it's a great book. Personal journaling as a way of getting rid of stuff before you go to write is also highly recommended.

Linda: Lulu.com is my favourite. I'd also recommend starting a wordpress.com blog and joining in with the writing community you will find there.

Just to add a little about Lulu.com – which is where and how my first book was published – it is a print-on-demand and distribution company. It's not the only one out there, but it has a fantastic range of resources available. There is much information on the website about formatting a book for print and digital distribution to sites like iStore, for instance. It can get your book into international distribution, and yet if you are in the UK you can be paid in pounds.

All these resources and more are listed in the **Resources** section which follows this chapter. So there is nothing further for me to add. I hope you have found this book useful and inspiring. Please do let me know how you get on; I love books and will look forward to reading yours.

> "If you wish to be a writer; write!"
>
> - Epicetus

12

Resources

Further Explanations

Partnership Publishing

Partnership publishing is a service offered by some publishers where you purchase a package which includes some of the services more usually associated with the traditional publishing route. This might include editing, creation of a book cover and some assistance with promotion. For examples of this type of service see Penn Press who are based in the UK (penpress.net/Full_Publication.html) and Morgan James Publishing (publishing.morgan-james.com/services/) based in the USA.

Amazon Advantage Program

The Amazon Advantage Program allows self-publishers to supply books directly to Amazon for them to keep in stock. This differs from Print-on-Demand and is for those who have their own print run. Amazon will determine the stock level they wish to have based on sales and will order books as required. This allows your book to have the all-important 'ships within 24 hours' status showing on the Amazon listings. See advantage.amazon.co.uk/gp/vendor/public/browse-main for more details in the UK and amazon.com/gp/seller-account/mm-product-page.html for more details inthe USA.

Distribution

Distribution is the act of allowing your books to be bought in the broadest of marketplaces, both online and offline (in bookshops). In the UK, this means using the two biggest book wholesalers, Gardners and Bertams. To use a distribution network your book must have an ISBN number which can be purchased in blocks of ten from Nielsen's in the UK. If you decide to use Lulu or another print on demand service, you can receive a free ISBN number, however this may mean that your book is considered published in another country and there may be tax implications.

Books

The Shortest Distance Between You and a Published Book by Susan Page

Writing Successful Self-Help and How To Books by Jean-Marie Stine

On Writing by Stephen King

Solutions for Writers by Sol Stein

Oxford A-Z of Grammar and Punctuation by John Seely

Never Die Wondering and *Get Cracking* by Wendy Knee

The Frugal Book Promoter by Carolyn Howard-Johnson

Plug Your Book by Steve Weber

Aiming At Amazon by Aaron Shepard

1001 Ways to Market Your Books by John Kremer

Websites

www.anneorchard.co.uk - home of the author's wordpress.com blog

www.womanontheedgeofreality.com - for hints, tips and resources for writers

www.Lulu.com - for print-on-demand and distribution services. Download a free resource, *Publish Your Book on a Shoestring Using Lulu Print on Demand* from www.anneorchard.co.uk

www.mslexia.co.uk - magazine and website for women who write

www.writers-forum.com - UK creative writing magazine

www.bookmarket.com - Book Marketing Website from John Kremer, author of *1001 Ways to Market Your Book*

www.charmouthliteraryfestival.org.uk - a one-day festival in South West England, for people who write

www.xmind.net - mind mapping software

www.gardners.com Book Wholesale UK

www.bertrams.com - Bertram Book Wholesale UK

www.nielsenbookdata.co.uk - Providers of UK ISBN Numbers

About The Author

Anne Orchard wanted to write a book for years. The trouble was she didn't know what it should be about, or who it was for. Finally she got the inspiration she needed – to write for the friends and family members of people with cancer; helping them address their own issues and so find it easier to be supporters. Self-published in 2008, *Their Cancer – Your Journey* was the result.

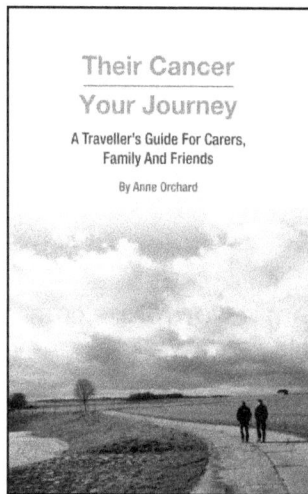

Their Cancer

Your Journey

A Traveller's Guide For Carers, Family And Friends

By Anne Orchard

When someone you care about is diagnosed with cancer, it forces you into an emotional journey too. How will you find your way? This book will be your guide.

With practical advice, as well as guidance on how to take your own inner journey, Anne shows you how to deal with this challenge in your life. You, too, can tap into your deepest strength and come through this ordeal with hope for the future.

Crystal Clear Books

Crystal Clear Books is a new and very small publishing company based in Dorset in the UK. Originally set up to act as the publisher for books by Linda Parkinson-Hardman it is slowly branching out to include other authors and is particularly interested in books by female authors and women's health.

Acknowledgements

Thanks go as always to my husband Pete for his encouragement and practical help. I am grateful to the contributors who gave their valuable time to share their experiences with us.

Wendy Knee deserves a special mention for encouraging me to broaden the scope of this book to the format you see today, and for her work in founding the Charmouth Literary Festival, a hands-on one-day festival where you get to be literary too (see **www.charmouthliteraryfestival.org.uk**).

Once again Steve Graham gets a mention for providing a catalyst by once saying to me "If I had a pound for everyone who said to me that they would like to write a book but hasn't done it I would be a rich man." Or possibly it was "I would be able to buy a pint of beer," I can't be sure.

Also Linda Parkinson-Hardman who provided the detailed knowledge of what it takes to self-publish which has allowed my first book to be born. She has now stepped in as my esteemed publisher, for which I am extraordinarily grateful.